LOVE
Never Fails

Kenneth Copeland

Unless otherwise noted, all scripture is from the *King James Version* of the Bible.

Love Never Fails

ISBN-10 1-57562-094-4   30-0036
ISBN-13 978-1-57562-094-7

19 18 17 16 15 14   29 28 27 26 25 24

© 1987 Eagle Mountain International Church Inc. aka Kenneth
Copeland Ministries

Kenneth Copeland Publications
Fort Worth, TX 76192-0001

For more information about Kenneth Copeland Ministries, visit kcm.org
or call 1-800-600-7395 (U.S. only) or +1-817-852-6000.

Love Never Fails

Fear of failure. It has haunted all of us at some time in our lives. Popular psychology advises us to adjust, learn to live with it. After all, failure is, to a certain extent, inevitable—isn't it?

Business statistics show eight out of 10 new businesses will close their doors within the first two years. More than 50 percent of today's marriages will collapse long before the "death do us part" vow is ever fulfilled. And yet the bulk of our failures never show up in such statistics. They hide themselves in the fabric of daily life... little failures on the job or with friends and family that break our hearts one tiny piece at a time and keep us from being the successes we always hoped to be.

But the Bible tells us there *is* a failure-proof way to live. It is the way of love. First Corinthians 13:8 says it plainly: "Love never fails."

Now, to those who think love expresses itself through emotion, that may sound silly. Emotion can't turn failure into success! But real love isn't expressed through emotion—it shows up in action. And the right action can make all the difference.

If you want to see an example of that kind of love in action, read the story recorded in Matthew 14. There, Jesus faces one of the toughest situations in His earthly ministry. If He responds in anger (as you and I would probably do), His ministry will end in failure. But by acting in love, He turns tragedy into success. Read verses 6-14:

> When Herod's birthday was kept, the daughter of Herodias danced before them, and pleased Herod.

Whereupon he promised with an oath to give her whatsoever she would ask. And she, being before instructed of her mother, said, Give me here John Baptist's head in a charger. And the king was sorry: nevertheless for the oath's sake, and them which sat with him at meat, he commanded it to be given her. And he sent, and beheaded John in the prison. And his head was brought in a charger, and given to the damsel: and she brought it to her mother. And his disciples came, and took up the body, and buried it, and went and told Jesus. When Jesus heard of it, he departed thence by ship into a desert place apart: and when the people had heard thereof, they followed him on foot out of the cities. And Jesus went forth, and saw a great multitude, and was moved with compassion toward them, and he healed their sick.

To get accurate insight into this situation, you must realize that John the Baptist had a closer kinship to Jesus in ministry than anyone else. John was not only His cousin, but a Spirit-anointed prophet who understood Jesus far better than Jesus' immediate family or anyone else on earth. He saw Jesus through the eyes of ministry.

When Jesus came to him at the Jordan River to be baptized, John, by the Holy Spirit, recognized who He was and said, "I shouldn't baptize You, You should baptize me." At that point, John was the only one who knew who Jesus was and what He was called of God to do.

Jesus dearly loved John and was blessed because of him. He once said, "Never was there a greater prophet born of a woman than this man" (see Luke 7:28). You could tell by the way Jesus talked that John meant a great deal to Him.

So you can imagine how Jesus felt when the disciples reported to Him that John had been brutally murdered—not for political reasons, but the result of a drunken party. He was murdered at the request of an immoral woman because some ol' boy shot his drunken mouth off! His head was brought on a plate and displayed publicly. What a mockery!

What would you do in such an emotionally taxing, grief-filled situation? Probably the same thing Jesus did. When He heard the news, He went out to be alone.

But then something very strange happened. When the people learned that Jesus was out there, they followed Him.

What would your response have been at that instant? I've often thought what I might have done. Most likely, I would have said, "Can't you people *ever* leave me alone? Can't I be alone just once without a bunch of people crowding me everywhere I go?" But that is not what Jesus did.

The Bible says Jesus was moved with compassion and healed their sick. He was not moved with grief over John. He was not moved with self-pity. He was not even moved with anger against Herod. Jesus was only moved with compassion. Why? Because He knew in the spirit realm that Satan was the real enemy in this situation.

I used to wonder why Jesus never retaliated—why He could just drop it and go on. What I didn't realize was that *Jesus did retaliate!* He overcame the works of Satan with compassion. He defeated hatred with love.

Jesus knew Herod was not really the one who had killed John. He was just a puppet. Satan was the one pulling the strings. So Jesus attacked Satan in the spirit realm by destroying his works—

the works of sickness and disease. He attacked pain and suffering with the compassion of God and healed and delivered those who were afflicted by the devil. Jesus retaliated against the real enemy, Satan. Don't you know that launching such an attack against Satan's kingdom was satisfying to Jesus!

You see, Jesus walked in the spirit. He saw into the other realm—into a world more real than the one which can only be seen with the physical eye. He stepped into that realm and did extensive damage to Satan's kingdom by being moved with the compassion of God.

Compassion doesn't just strike at the surface of things or relieve outward symptoms. Compassion goes to the root of the problem: the devil and his works. When you learn to be motivated by God's compassion, you realize that people are not your enemy. When people come against you with persecution, affliction and accusations to harass you and make your life miserable, launch your attack against Satan because he is the real enemy.

If Jesus had allowed Satan to force Him into retaliating in the area of human emotions, He would have been trapped into physical warfare, which would have ruined His ministry. Operating in the flesh profits nothing. The Bible says our warfare is not against flesh and blood, but against principalities, powers, rulers of the darkness of this world, and spiritual wickedness in high places (Ephesians 6:12).

How could Jesus react in love in such a murderous situation? Because He was moved by the Holy Spirit of God—*Compassion* Himself. He was motivated by love. He reacted the way love would react. God *is* love (1 John 4:8), and Jesus always did only what the Father, who is Love, told Him to do. Compassion is a person. Compassion is God Himself.

"But that was Jesus!" you say. "He had a direct line to the Father. I don't!" Oh, yes you do! You have the ability, through the same Holy Spirit who indwelt Jesus, to be moved with compassion, just as He was. Romans 5:5 tells us that the love of God is shed abroad in *our* hearts by the Holy Spirit. All we have to do is make the decision to be motivated by His love rather than our own human feelings.

Love is not a feeling, and a feeling is not the evidence of love. Love is a person, and action is the evidence of it. When the Bible says that Jesus was moved with compassion, it could have said He was moved by God, not a feeling. Compassion—the Father—sent Him into the world, not to condemn it but to save it, praise God! Regardless of what people did to Him, Jesus was only moved with compassion for them.

Someone might say, "Well, if *I* did

that, people would walk all over me. If I turned the other cheek every time I was slapped, I'd be beaten to a pulp." That's the way the world and most Christians think because they don't understand the principle behind turning the other cheek.

Do you remember when Jesus went back to Nazareth and the religious folks were so angry with Him they wanted to push Him off a cliff? What happened? The Bible says He just walked right through that hostile crowd. He didn't hit anyone or call fire down from heaven on them. He just walked right past them, and no one could lay a finger on Him. Another time they decided to stone Him, and He didn't retaliate that time either. He just walked off. No one could touch Him.

I asked the Lord how it was possible for Jesus to avoid confrontation without the crowd becoming violent and without being killed or stoned. He reminded me of Ephesians 6:16 which says that the shield of faith would quench all the fiery darts of the wicked one. *All* the darts— not just 75 percent of them!

When we are walking in the love of God, being moved by compassion, a supernatural shield of faith protects us from all the fiery darts of the wicked. And the key to keeping that shield in place lies in keeping and obeying God's Word. Notice 1 John 2:5: "But whoso keepeth his word, in him verily is the love of God perfected."

What does keeping God's Word have to do with living in love? To be motivated by love is to be moved not by feelings, but by God, by Compassion Himself. And God communicates Himself to us through His Word, so whatever the Word says to do, we just do it. We put God's Word first place in our lives. This is living in the love of God. Read 1 John 5:3 very carefully.

Love is perfected by putting the Word first place and the Bible says that love *never* fails. No matter what the situation looks like, it can't fail because God is love and God cannot fail. You don't have to be afraid of failure anymore. In fact, you don't have to be afraid of anything. As 1 John 4:18 says, "There is no fear in love; but perfect love casteth out fear."

So just take God at His Word. Act on it even when you don't feel like it. You can depend on God to back His Word and see to it that you don't fail.

When Jesus walked through that bloodthirsty crowd, He wasn't sneaking away as if He were afraid they might hurt Him. He knew they couldn't touch Him because He was walking in the protection of God. No one could harm Him until He laid His life down as the Lamb slain for the sins of the world. Jesus told Herod, "You can't take My life. It's Mine to pick up or to lay down, and no man can take it from Me."

When Jesus said to turn the other cheek, He didn't mean that you would have to stand there and have your brains beaten out. If you are keeping the Word, you can expect a man to swing at you and not be able to hit you!

Nicky Cruz's testimony is a perfect example of this. Nicky was reputed to be the most ruthless gang leader of his time. And when David Wilkerson, the man who led Nicky to the Lord, stood in front of him, telling him about Jesus, Nicky thrust his knife at David several times, trying to kill him. Every time he did, David just said, "Nicky, you can cut me into a thousand pieces and every piece will say, 'I love you and God loves you.'" Because of love, Nicky couldn't get his knife close enough to David to hurt him. A supernatural force always stopped it short. My friend, love *never* fails!

Love unconditionally by acting on

God's Word, loving God by loving others, walking in love, perfecting the love walk. Think about it, meditate on it and keep the other promises of God. They'll all work too, because faith worketh by love (Galatians 5:6). So does joy, peace, patience and the other parts of the fruit of the spirit. If you'll walk on that commandment of love, all the other promises of God begin to work. The Bible says, "Whereby are given unto us exceeding great and precious promises: that by these ye might be partakers of the divine nature…" (2 Peter 1:4).

Confessing and acting on the exceeding great and precious promises of His Word, you become a partaker of His divine nature. That is when you begin to see the miraculous take place in your family. Jesus said the storms of life have no power to destroy your house when you're a doer of the Word. (Read Luke 6:46-49.)

Love is the greatest thing that could

ever happen to your family. If the devil has stolen your husband from you, or your wife or your children, you can win them to Jesus with the love of God.

Love is the greatest thing that could ever happen to your business, too. A friend of mine went into a television and radio business and wanted to buy a station from a Jewish man. He told him, "The Word of God says that if I will bless you, God will bless me. So I'm going to see to it that you get the better part of this deal." Most people would have been afraid to say such a thing. They'd be afraid of being taken advantage of.

But that deal turned out to be exceptionally profitable for both of them. My friend was a tremendous Christian witness to his Jewish friend, and they ended up preaching the gospel of Jesus Christ together on radio. When love rules, prosperity can flow.

So, commit to living the life of the love of God today by determining to obey the

Word, no matter what. Then watch God turn failure into success again and again at home, at work, in any situation. You can prove it for yourself—love never fails!

Prayer for Salvation and Baptism in the Holy Spirit

Heavenly Father, I come to You in the Name of Jesus. Your Word says, "Whosoever shall call on the name of the Lord shall be saved" (Acts 2:21). I am calling on You. I pray and ask Jesus to come into my heart and be Lord over my life according to Romans 10:9-10: "If thou shalt confess with thy mouth the Lord Jesus, and shalt believe in thine heart that God hath raised him from the dead, thou shalt be saved. For with the heart man believeth unto righteousness; and with the mouth confession is made unto salvation." I do that now. I confess that Jesus is Lord, and I believe in my heart that God raised Him from the dead. I repent of sin. I renounce it. I renounce the devil and everything he stands for. Jesus is my Lord.

I am now reborn! I am a Christian—a child of Almighty God! I am saved! You also said in Your Word, "If ye then, being evil, know how to give good gifts unto your children: HOW MUCH MORE shall your heavenly Father give the Holy Spirit to them that ask him?" (Luke 11:13). I'm also asking You to fill me with the Holy Spirit. Holy Spirit, rise up within me as I praise God. I fully expect to speak with other tongues as You give me the utterance (Acts 2:4). In Jesus' Name. Amen!

Begin to praise God for filling you with the Holy Spirit. Speak those words and syllables you receive—not in your own language, but the language given to you by the Holy Spirit. You have to use your own voice. God will not force you to speak. Don't be concerned with how it sounds. It is a heavenly language!

Continue with the blessing God has given you and pray in the spirit every day.

You are a born-again, Spirit-filled believer. You'll never be the same!

Find a good church that boldly preaches God's Word and obeys it. Become part of a church family who will love and care for you as you love and care for them.

We need to be connected to each other. It increases our strength in God. It's God's plan for us.

Make it a habit to watch the Believer's Voice of Victory Network television broadcast and become a doer of the Word, who is blessed in his doing (James 1:22-25).

About the Author

Kenneth Copeland is co-founder and president of Kenneth Copeland Ministries in Fort Worth, Texas, and best-selling author of books that include *Honor— Walking in Honesty, Truth and Integrity,* and *THE BLESSING of The LORD Makes Rich and He Adds No Sorrow With It.*

Since 1967, Kenneth has been a minister of the gospel of Christ and teacher of God's WORD. He is also the artist on award-winning albums such as his Grammy-nominated *Only the Redeemed, In His Presence, He Is Jehovah, Just a Closer Walk* and *Big Band Gospel.* He also co-stars as the character Wichita Slim in the children's adventure videos *The Gunslinger, Covenant Rider* and the movie *The Treasure of Eagle Mountain,* and as Daniel Lyon in the Commander Kellie and the Superkids™ videos *Armor of Light* and *Judgment: The Trial of Commander Kellie.* Kenneth also co-stars as a Hispanic godfather in the 2009 and 2016 movies *The Rally* and *The Rally 2: Breaking the Curse.*

With the help of offices and staff in the United States, Canada, England, Australia, South Africa, Ukraine, Singapore and Latin America Kenneth is fulfilling his vision to boldly preach the uncompromised WORD of God from the top of this world, to the bottom, and all the way around. His ministry reaches millions of people worldwide through daily and Sunday TV broadcasts, magazines, teaching audios and videos, conventions and campaigns, and the World Wide Web.

Learn more about Kenneth Copeland Ministries by visiting our website at kcm.org.

When The LORD first spoke to Kenneth and Gloria Copeland about starting the *Believer's Voice of Victory* magazine...

He said: *This is your seed. Give it to everyone who ever responds to your ministry, and don't ever allow anyone to pay for a subscription!*

For more than 40 years, it has been the joy of Kenneth Copeland Ministries to bring the good news to believers. Readers enjoy teaching from ministers who write from lives of living contact with God, and testimonies from believers experiencing victory through God's Word in their everyday lives.

Today, the *BVOV* magazine is mailed monthly, bringing encouragement and blessing to believers around the world. Many even use it as a ministry tool, passing it on to others who desire to know Jesus and grow in their faith!

Request your FREE subscription to the *Believer's Voice of Victory* magazine today!

Go to **freevictory.com** to subscribe, or call us at
1-800-600-7395 (U.S. only) or **+1-817-852-6000**.

We're Here for You!®

Your growth in God's WORD and victory in Jesus are at the very center of our hearts. In every way God has equipped us, we will help you deal with the issues facing you, so you can be the **victorious overcomer** He has planned for you to be.

The mission of Kenneth Copeland Ministries is about all of us growing and going together. Our prayer is that you will take full advantage of all The LORD has given us to share with you.

Wherever you are in the world, you can watch the *Believer's Voice of Victory* broadcast on television (check your local listings), the Internet at kcm.org or on our digital Roku channel.

Our website, **kcm.org,** gives you access to every resource we've developed for your victory. And, you can find contact information for our international offices in Africa, Asia, Australia, Canada, Europe, Ukraine and our headquarters in the United States.

Each office is staffed with devoted men and women, ready to serve and pray with you. You can contact the worldwide office nearest you for assistance, and you can call us for prayer at our U.S. number, +1-817-852-6000, 24 hours every day!

We encourage you to connect with us often and let us be part of your everyday walk of faith!

Jesus Is LORD!

Kenneth & Gloria Copeland

Kenneth and Gloria Copeland